techniques of Typography

techniques of
Typography

by Cal Swann

Lund Humphries, London

Acknowledgements

This book is dedicated to Tom Westley

My thanks are due to the considerable help given by Tony Bennett, who set nearly all the letterpress exercises and made many constructive suggestions, and to Ivan Osborne, who did all the photography (with the exception of the film matrix case supplied by The Monotype Corporation).
Also to Stan Warford, who read the proofs, to John George and other staff of the School of Printing of Manchester College of Art & Design, the Monotype Corporation Limited, Linotype and Machinery Limited, and IBM (UK) Limited.

Contents

Contents (continued)

We are no longer obliged to marshal an army of lead in order to march our ideas into print. Photography and the new techniques of reproduction which it has inspired have released typography from the straight-jacket of metal type composition. This freedom from mechanical restriction provides the designer with wonderful opportunities for producing imaginative and sympathetic visual solutions. But although the use of metal type in printing is diminishing, conventional letterpress will continue to be used on a considerable scale for many kinds of work for many years to come. A thorough understanding of the constraints of conventional typography is therefore of practical importance and also enables the designer to recognize and to grasp the opportunities presented by the new techniques of composition.

'The new book', said Lissitzky, 'demands new writers'. In *Techniques of Typography* Cal Swann has not only described the variety of ways in which today the word may be conveyed into print but, significantly in a book which deals with techniques of alphabetic communication, he has done so with the minimum use of words. The result is an exceptionally clear introduction to contemporary typographical methods and a demonstration which allows the 'reader' to experience something of the pleasure, the excitement and the satisfaction which surrounds the production of the printed word, whatever means are employed.

Herbert Spencer

Printing methods are increasingly diversifying and expanding from the established letterpress equipment into offset-lithography and photo-gravure, while the techniques of preparing originals for photographic reproduction are similarly developing with the wider use of filmsetting and transfer lettering systems. It is hoped, by showing very clearly the technical restrictions of the typographic method, to discourage the unfortunate mimicry of the compositor's limitations practised by graphic artists preparing artwork without these constraints. Letterforms cast as relief printing surfaces on square metal bodies do not necessarily produce the ideal visual result and the freedom to produce such a result with the new methods now available is being hampered by the adherence to ideas applicable primarily to conventional typography.

This book is intended for printing apprentices, design students and graphic artists in commercial studios as a guide to the purely visual aspects of typographic design. It does not set out to examine the message to be communicated, only the techniques by which the words themselves may be visually presented as a printed image.

The problems of composition for continuous reading have been adequately covered in numerous books on type and legibility and although a section is included on text setting the points raised here are mainly concerned with the visual refinements necessary for 'display' settings.

The most common form of printing is by the process known as letterpress. A shape is cut or moulded so that it becomes a surface standing out in relief. This is inked by a roller, paper is placed on top and pressure applied to transfer the ink on to the paper. The relief 'image' must be cut in reverse so that when it prints it is the correct way round. Linocuts, wood-cuts, etc, are examples of relief printing surfaces.

In commercial printing, combinations of type, photo-engraved blocks (plates), etc, may be composed together, as typographic material is manufactured to specific dimensions on a scale which in the USA and Great Britain is known as the Anglo-American Point System.

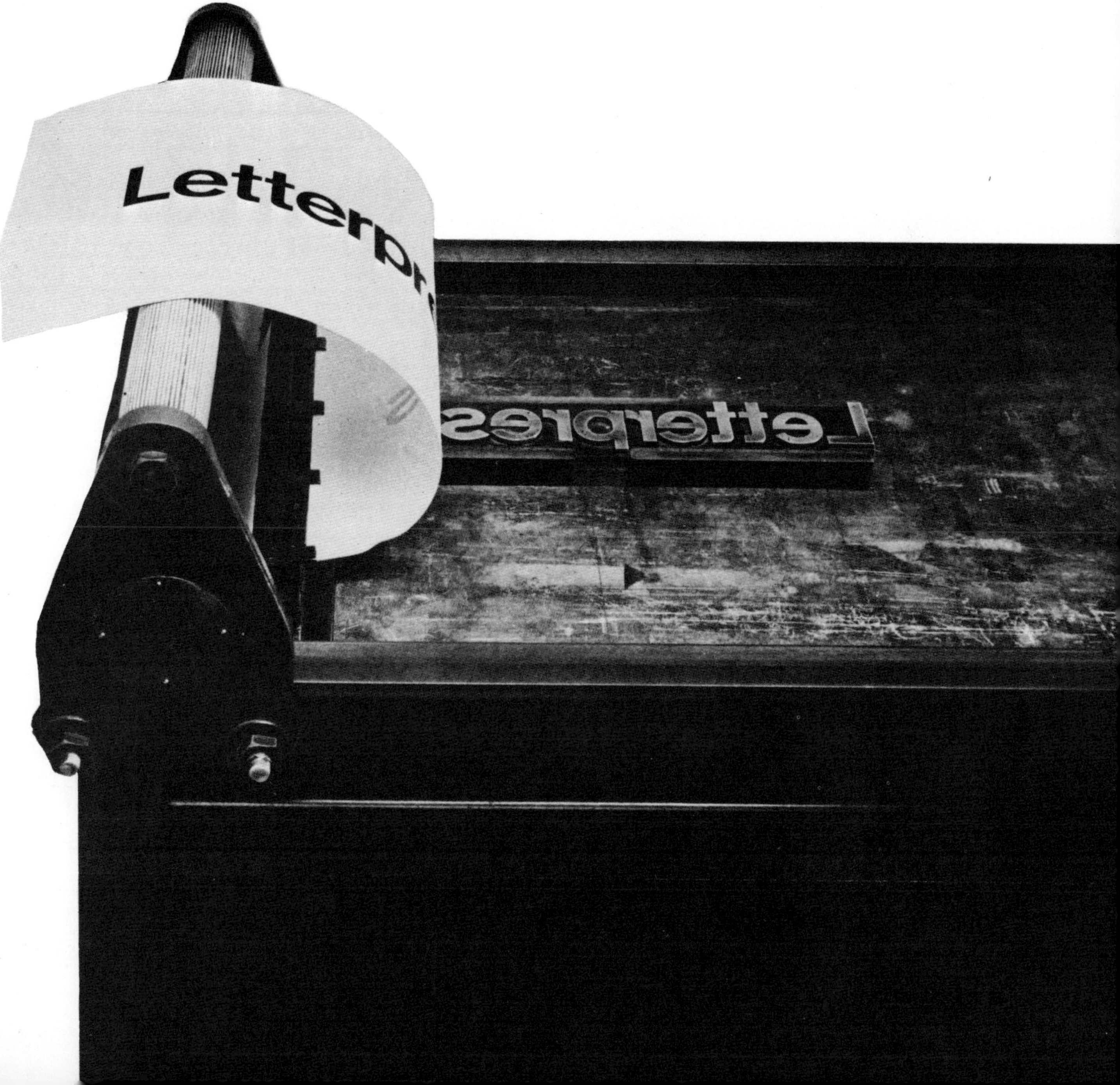
Letterpr

Lithography is a means of printing from a flat surface and is achieved by making use of the natural reaction between grease and water. The original lithographers printed from a stone, but today in commercial work the image is applied to a zinc plate by chemicals which fix it to the desired areas. To print, the plate is first dampened and then rolled with ink which only adheres to the portions chemically prepared to receive it; the wet areas of the plate repel the greasy ink. Paper is fed to the plate and pressure is applied to transfer the image on to the paper. In commercial work, the image is 'offset' on to a rubber blanket before being impressed on to the paper.

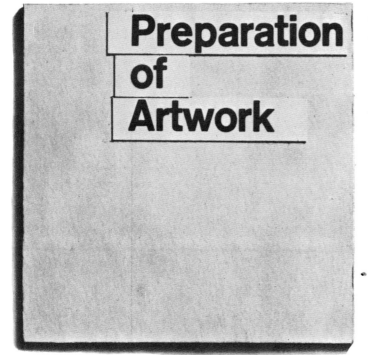

To make a relief printing surface other than from metal type, the image must be suitably prepared for photography. This prepared material is referred to as artwork. It may be composed of lettering, proofs of typematter, drawings, photographs, etc, which are mounted or drawn in black ink on white board. The sample above is composed of proofs of typeset matter known as 'reproduction proofs'. These must be of good quality, because any small blemishes are reproduced by the camera. Artwork needs to be prepared with precision and cleanliness, showing a clear distinction between the black image and the white background.

A negative is made in a camera using film which is sensitive only to the white areas on the artwork and leaves the black areas totally opaque. Shadows from patches on the original artwork and any other faults in the negative may be removed by painting out with opaque retouching fluid.

Photographs showing numerous tones between black and white are reproduced in much the same way, but the negative is broken up into minute dots by inserting a screen between the camera lens and the negative. The varying density of the dots creates an optical effect of different tones of grey.

Preparation of Artwork

A metal plate is chemically treated with a light-sensitive emulsion and the negative is placed in contact with it. The plate is exposed to light. This cannot pass through the opaque areas (white areas on the original) but does pass through the clear parts of the negative (black areas on the original) and hardens the emulsion on the plate. This is then washed to remove the unexposed emulsion. After further chemical treatment with an acid resist to protect the emulsion left behind, the plate is etched in an acid bath and the image is left standing as a relief surface. This is referred to as a line block (plate) and is mounted on to wood or light metal to bring it to the same height as type for printing. The negative broken up into dots representing tones ranging from white to black is used to make a relief surface known as a half-tone block (plate).

The block (plate) is printed with or without other typographic material by inking the surface and making an impression on paper. Letterpress half-tone blocks (plates) require a very smooth paper surface in order to print the fine screen of dots adequately. Litho-offset plates can also carry either line or half-tone subjects. Since the image is transferred via a soft rubber blanket, however, it can make use of a greater variety of paper surfaces for half-tone subjects. In photo-lithography, all the copy is prepared as artwork and a negative made in the same way as in making a block (plate) for letterpress but the negative is photographically transferred to the flat litho plate.

The term 'display' refers to those larger type sizes which are usually used for headings and display. Filmsetting machines which are intended for this type of work are based either on the 'contact' or 'enlarger' photographic principles. The contact machines produce a print at the same size as the negative and are normally operated by automatic spacing and alignment controls which may be adjusted to increase or close up the spacing. Those machines based on the normal photographic enlarger are capable of visual spacing and can produce a print at any size from $\frac{1}{4}$ to 3 inches from the same negative. Various lenses can also be attached to compress, extend, slope, etc, the original letterform.

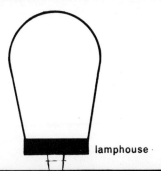

negative

£ $ ¢ » « / : . , - ¿ i = ¨ ˜ A B C D E F G H I J K L M N O P Q R S T U V W X Y Z Ç Æ Œ + ´ ` ˆ ? ! „ " &

1 2 3 4 5 6 7 8 9 0 * ˊ × ˝ ˜ a b c d e f g h i j k l m n o p q r s t u v w x y z ç æ œ ı ´ ` ( ) ' ß °/₀

lens

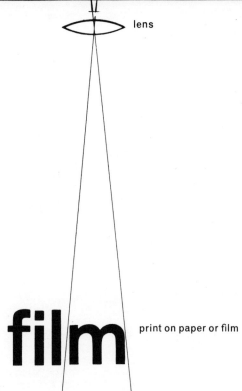

film

print on paper or film

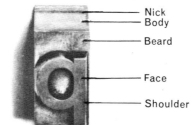

Nick
Body

Beard

Face

Shoulder

Point
size of
type

The typographic image is formed from individual characters which are
set (composed) together to form words. The Face is the engraved
image which is inked and comes into contact with the paper; either side
of the face is the Shoulder (or bevel) which leads to the Body (or
shank) of the type itself. The height from the Foot of the type to the
Face is 0·918 inch and all the dimensions of type are measured in the
Anglo-American Point System, one point being 0·0138 inch. 12 points
make one 'em' (or Pica) and 6 ems (or 72 points) are roughly equivalent
to 1 inch.
The Beard is the term given to the space at the bottom of the face
which accommodates the 'descenders' in lower-case types and the
Nick enables the compositor readily to identify which way up the letter is.
The set is the width across the letter.

Hxy   Hxy

The sizes of metal type faces are given in terms of the vertical body measurement (in points). The printed image (derived from faces which are nominally the same size) may, however, vary in apparent size. This is due to the differing proportions of the ascenders and descenders in relation to the size of the lower-case 'x'.

The metal body point size has been the most convenient means of standardization in the typographic system but it can mean that 10pt in some typefaces may look as big as 12pt in others. A visual standard is now feasible in filmsetting, although the metal body point sizes have in practice been followed literally throughout.

printing height (0.918″)

Printing surfaces must be the same height and the non-printing areas must be made up of material which is at a lower height than the printing surfaces. This spacing material is made of lead, light alloy or plastic, but must be made to dimensions on the point scale. All measurements above 12 points can be expressed in terms of 12pt ems (known as pica ems) and the illustration above shows side elevation, elevation and plan view of a line of 24pt type and spaces at 22 ems length, bounded by a 6pt × 22 ems 'lead' and a 2 em × 22 em piece of plastic 'furniture'. 'Leads' and 'furniture' are examples of spacing material.

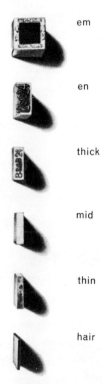

em

en

thick

mid

thin

hair

Each typeface in a composing room is contained in a flat case sub-divided into small boxes to take a quantity of each letter, the figures and the various spaces. In every size of type, the spacing system is identical; the Em space (not to be confused with the Pica em) is a square unit of the vertical body point size. Two Ens equal one Em, three Thicks equal one Em, four Mids equal one Em and five Thins equal one Em. The hair space is theoretically twelve to the Em but in practice is of varying thicknesses (eg. 1pt, 2pt, 3pt, etc) and used for very fine adjustments of space.

d

d

Garalde

(Old Face c.1500)

Transitional Roman

(c.1750)

Didone

(Modern Face c.1800)

Modern (bracketed serifs)

Fat Face

Garalde (referred to as 'Old Face' or 'Old Style') types were in use shortly after the invention of printing and were modelled on the 'humanist' pen-written letterform popular at that time.

The derivation from the pen-drawn character therefore gives it the angled serifs (the 'tails' at the ends of straight strokes) and sloped axis of the round shapes which are made naturally with the square-nibbed pen.

The 'Transitional Roman' typefaces were developed by the mid-eighteenth century and have a more vertical stress with less reliance on the pen-made shapes.

The Didone or 'Modern' letter was fully developed by the end of the eighteenth century and shows a letterform which is entirely typographic in concept, derived from the engraving tools of the punch-cutter.

The serifs are sometimes fine hair lines and the thickening of the round forms is vertically biased; this letterform also lends itself to variations in thickness without destroying its basic character, and the serifs may be 'bracketed' (curved into the main stroke).

The wide variety of typefaces available are difficult to classify, because many designs have characteristics which are common to more than any one group. The chart below shows the four principal categories in type design and the derivation from these of the most common sub groups. There are numerous historic and decorative letterforms which fall outside this classification but this covers the normal range of faces in constant use.

d

Lineale

(c.1830)

Grotesque

d

Slab Serif

(Egyptian c.1830)

Clarendon

(Bracketed serif)

A 'sanserif' or Lineale type first made its appearance in 1816 but it did not become popular until the 1830s when its versatile character answered the growing demand for 'display' types.

The main features are the absence of serifs and an apparent even thickness of the strokes. The lack of decoration – serifs – and its anonymous character have been the reasons for the extensive use of this group of types by modern graphic designers as the most suitable letterform for speed of communication.

The slab (or square) serif types came into use at about the same time as the Lineale and were termed 'Egyptian' largely due to their initial association with exhibitions of Egyptian antiquity.

The serifs are slab-like strokes similar in thickness to the main strokes of the letter which are also like the sanserif in their uniform weight. This group shares too the adaptability of the Lineale in the variety of weights, etc, and the serifs may be bracketed, as in the Clarendons.

CAPS
AND

The height of capital letters usually equals that of the letters with ascenders, and passages set in capitals inevitably leave a space between each line which is dictated by the beard on the type. The beard can be cut off the metal, but this is time-consuming and costly and this effect is usually achieved by proofing the lines, cutting out the space and pasting up in position to reproduce photographically.

TITLING FOUNTS

There are some typefaces which are intended for setting titles only. These types are composed entirely of capitals and there is no beard. Such faces are known as titling founts (fonts).

set width

Typefounders cast their letterforms on the metal body to allow the lower-case letters to combine as evenly as possible. The shoulder left on either side of the face is a compromise to take account of letters that look close together, 'in , 'lm', etc, and widely spaced letters such as 'ry', 'tw', etc.

The amount of space between letters in a word is related to the counters, or open spaces enclosed within the letterforms. If these are open and generous, then the spaces should be in proportion. Unfortunately, in display sizes many types suffer from an excessive shoulder on the type. Words are read as complete shapes and excessive letterspacing does not help the perception of this whole shape.

set width

The intelligent use of filmsetting and transfer lettering systems which allows designers to space words visually and compactly has influenced some typefounders to cast their display founts (fonts) to set much closer together.

The letters of Grotesque No. 2 (Series 51) on the page opposite are too widely spaced at this size and a comparison with Standard, above, demonstrates the advantage of a compact setting,

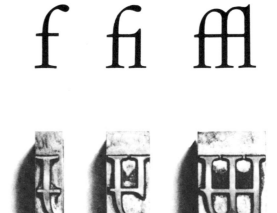

There are a number of letterforms which overlap the following letter in order to fit closely together and these are usually supplied by the type-founder with each fount (font).
The projection of the 'f' overhangs its body width and rests on the following letter and this feature is known as a 'kern'. When the following letter happens to be another f, i or l, the characters are designed and cast on one metal body and are known as ligatures.

Italics and scripts

Some italic founts (fonts) and scripts are cast on a sloping body in order to set compactly and there are often more ligatures to imitate the cursive, handwritten effect.

fffffffff f film

The technique of filmsetting is obviously not subject to the same limitation as the rectangular metal type bodies. The letterform produced from a master film negative can be overprinted or allowed to overhang the next letter to fit visually. The design of the individual characters must avoid overprints which do not 'register' as with the lower-case f and i.

set width

set width

set width

The word spacing of film set characters is also capable of greater variation than in normal typesetting as the few examples above show. Most display filmsetters can easily set letters so tight that they touch or overlap, and even the alignment can be raised or lowered. Many more effects may be achieved with the application of distortion lenses and/or by inserting screens between the negative and photographic surface.

Typography

Combinations of capital and lower-case letters often present awkward gaps as demonstrated above. The solution when artwork is being prepared is to cut the proof and slot the letters closer together. Most display filmsetters and transfer lettering systems can be visually spaced and do not need to imitate the 'holes' caused by the mechanics of the metal type process.

Typography

The larger point sizes of type can be mortised (cut away so as to interlock) as shown above. This overcomes the difficult letter combinations but is obviously not practical in smaller sizes.
A few typefaces are supplied with special ligatures of the capital 'T' and 'Y', etc, which have a number of following letter combinations cast on the same body with the spacing corrected.

TYPOGRAPHY

The capital founts (fonts) are also cast by the typefounders to combine as evenly as possible with the lower-case letters and when capitals are set together, the shapes of the letters leave considerably more uneven spaces between them. The ideal word shape to read is visually even and compact. Hand-drawn letters made up into words can be modified to overcome the gaps. In preparing artwork from type pulls, filmsetting or 'Letraset', etc, the letters can be adjusted to appear visually correct by overlapping or shortening parts of the letters.

TYPOGRAPHY

Metal letters cannot easily be closed up and the alternative is to increase the space between those letters which appear too close to match the apparent large areas of white space which some characters inevitably leave. The amount of space to insert obviously varies and the differences may entail cutting special 'spaces' out of cardboard or paper before the compositor is satisfied. Therefore it is usually the important titles and phrases only which are treated in this costly manner, and where letterspacing is required in smaller sizes it is seldom 'visual' but an even fixed space throughout the line.

CONDENSED TYPES ARE WEAKENED BY LETTERSPACING

The practice of letterspacing has been a traditional skill of the compositor but it can be carried to excess – opening out the words emphasizes the individual letters and not necessarily the word shape which is what the eye should perceive.
Condensed letterforms were designed to allow more words to be contained in a line while retaining a large height for emphasis. It is hardly logical to letterspace such faces and the effect of doing so is to weaken the horizontal strength of words and lines.

LETTERS MAY BE CUT AND OVERPRINTED TO MAKE COMPACT LINES

It is important with condensed letters which have small white counters that the space between them is also small. Tight word spacing poses problems with type as has been demonstrated, but the example above has been set in Letraset and characters such as 'TT' have been cut and closed up. These slight modifications to the letterforms help the word shape without the character of the letterform being lost – too great an alteration draws attention to itself and legibility suffers.

Justification of lines to square measures inevitably requires varying spaces on each line

In order to be capable of manipulation, lines of type must conform to the standard range of spacing material on the point system; consequently the composing 'stick' is pre-set to a suitable length measured in ems. When this measure is filled, the word spaces are adjusted as evenly as possible throughout the line to fit the measure tightly and each line is 'justified' in this manner.

In lines of normal continuous reading, containing an average of nine to ten word spaces, this spacing discrepancy from line to line is hardly noticeable, but lines averaging seven words or less should not be justified. In such cases the gaps caused by justification severely disrupt the easy movement of the eye along the line and tend to associate words together vertically rather than horizontally.

An even visual word space is achieved when lines are set as so-called 'unjustified'

The alternative to justification is for the compositor to place a constant word space throughout the line and justify at the end. The type is still justified, in fact, but the term 'unjustified' has been widely used to describe this printed effect of a ragged right-hand edge; 'fixed word space' is a more accurate description. This practice has many advantages in providing a consistent reading speed and avoiding too many word breaks and it is reasonable to assume that the fixed word space is more functional and economical than justified lines, whatever their length. In display filmsetters, it is very difficult to justify. In most cases, the line has to be set twice before the required length is obtained.

Too much space between words hinders smooth reading by the spotty effect this has on the eye

The amount of space between words is proportionate to the amount of space between letters – where the letterspace is generous because of the character of the letterform, the word space is similarly more generous than in types of narrow width. The amount of space should not be more than is necessary to show a distinct difference between letter and word spacing. This break is surprisingly small and it is a common fault to exaggerate it.

The correct space varies according to the design of the letter form but a useful guideiisitheithicknessiof theilower-casei'i'iinitheitype sizeitoibeiused

The perceptive senses take in shapes which are related together by proximity and contour. We are taught to read our code system horizontally from left to right and it is primarily this 'conditioning' that enables the eye to follow badly spaced copy where the interlinear space appears less than that between words. The horizontal left to right movement can be clearly differentiated from the vertical downward movement by keeping the word space to a minimum.

Purely mechanical word spacing, although even, can create 'holes' which are visually disturbing

The irregularities in the design of letterforms which create spacing problems within words also give the appearance of extra space between some words and not others – especially the white space above punctuation marks. The compositor and graphic artist need to develop an appreciation of these peculiarities and automatically to counteract them.

In large sizes, word spaces need adjusting to appear visually even, particularly after punctuation

The optical differences in word spacing which show up in type sizes over 14pt can be corrected by reducing the actual space until the printed result looks even. As the compositor may find himself using filmsetters, etc, in the near future, mechanical rules of thumb derived from metal typesetting are not likely to offer much guidance; only an understanding of the basic visual relationships will enable the operator to utilize each machine to its full potential.

Optical adjustments required in leading

In continuous reading matter, the amount of space between the lines is related to the length of line, x-height of the type, etc, and this is dealt with in the section on 'typographic style for text composition'.
In display sizes, the optical effect of ascenders and descenders is similar to the apparent differences which occur in word spacing and some lines can look closer together than others. Lines which are set 'solid' or very closely spaced need very careful handling, as the space, if too narrow, can conflict with the word space which should always appear less than that between the lines.
The setting above has no 'leading' and is set 'solid'.

Optical adjustments required in leading

Inserting interlinear spacing material (made of lead in various point thicknesses and cut into lengths to em measures) helps to reduce the obvious unevenness but does not solve the problem if the same leading is used throughout. The setting above has an even 2pt lead inserted between each line.

Optical adjustments required in leading

To obtain a proof which looks correct, the setting above has (from the top) a 4pt lead, a 3pt lead, a 1pt lead, while the bottom two lines are left solid.
Settings in film or transfer lettering, etc, also need to be cut and repositioned until visually correct.

base line to ———

base line ———

Optical adjustments required in leading

In the case of metal type measurements taken from the base line of the x-height to the base line of the x-height of the line below obviously cannot be less than the point size of the type. The beard on the type can be cut off but this operation is not economical and normally there is no way of printing lines of type closer together. This is not the case in filmsetting as the negative may be exposed over a previous setting if desired. Point size and leading terminology has no real meaning in the field of filmsetting and measuring from base line to base line offers a more rational system.

LINING TYPE FLUSH LEFT

The compositor places type into the composing stick and justifies to an even measure. He usually aligns the letters simply by starting at the beginning of the stick. The shape of the letters can consequently leave visual 'holes' in the printed result.

LINING TYPE FLUSH LEFT

To align type so that it appears visually correct requires lines to be indented to take account of awkward letters that present holes. Where possible, these lines should be set first and the subsequent lines suitably indented.

In filmsetting and Letraset, etc, the letterforms may be visually aligned as they are set; certainly there is no reason for the visual alignment being incorrectly adjusted in any type of prepared artwork.

PUNCTUATION, PARTICULARLY IN RANGED RIGHT COPY, CREATES GAPS

The same refinements are necessary for copy that is ranged on the right as for that which is ranged left, punctuation at the ends of lines often causing the optically 'ragged' edge as shown above.

WIDER MEASURES ALLOW OPTICAL CORRECTIONS IN THE MARGIN

The compositor of display typesettings should anticipate alignment problems and set the lines indented appropriately to counter the visual spaces left by letterforms, punctuation, etc.

The Monotype system mechanically composes and justifies single type bodies (individual characters as distinct from lines or slugs set as one piece of metal) from $4\frac{1}{4}$pt to 14pt via a keyboard unit and a casting machine. The keyboard unit is basically an extended typewriter keyboard which produces a perforated paper ribbon that controls the movement of the matrix case in the casting machine.

The keyboard operator presets the unit for the required length of line and types out the copy. At the end of each line he taps the appropriate justification keys which he reads from a special scale. The casting machine is fitted with the correct matrix case and assembles the cast type in lines on a galley (shown opposite).

ABCDEFGHIJKLMNOPQRSTUVWXYZ
abcdefghijklmnopqrstuvwxyz£1234567890&.,:;-!?()[]——

ABCDEFGHIJKLMNOPQRSTUVWXYZ
abcdefghijklmnopqrstuvwxyz1234567890&.,:-!?

ABCDEFGHIJKLMNOPQRSTUVWXYZ
abcdefghijklmnopqrstuvwxyz£1234567890&.,;:-!?()—

ABCDEFGHIJKLMNOPQRSTUVWXYZ

The matrix case shown opposite contains 272 characters (including figures and punctuation) which generally allows for six or seven alphabets in any one size of type as shown above. These related founts (fonts), roman capitals and lower-case, italic capitals and lower-case, bold capitals and lower-case, and in most seriffed types also the small capitals can be set and cast with the minimum number of operations and it is therefore more economical to design text matter consisting of headings, sub-headings, etc, within the framework of these alphabets.

The depth of type cast on the 'Monotype' machine is measured in points in the conventional manner but the width is measured in 'units of set' points. The em quad in any 'Monotype' size is divided into eighteen units and is the basis for all the spacing and widths of the letterforms. This allows considerable refinements in both the letter-shapes and spacing of the lines of type.

The specimen opposite shows samples of 'Monotype' unit spacing, where the units have been cast on to the side of the type characters to achieve letterspacing. Extra depth can also be cast on the beard of the type to 'lead' text settings.

9 unit word space

no letterspace	LETTERSPACED ROMAN CAPITALS
1 unit letterspace	LETTERSPACED ROMAN CAPITALS
2 unit letterspace	LETTERSPACED ROMAN CAPITALS
3 unit letterspace	LETTERSPACED ROMAN CAPITALS

11 unit word space

1 unit letterspace	LETTERSPACED ROMAN CAPITALS
2 unit letterspace	LETTERSPACED ROMAN CAPITALS
3 unit letterspace	LETTERSPACED ROMAN CAPITALS

6 unit word space

no letterspace	LETTERSPACED SMALL CAPITALS
1 unit letterspace	LETTERSPACED SMALL CAPITALS
2 unit letterspace	LETTERSPACED SMALL CAPITALS
3 unit letterspace	LETTERSPACED SMALL CAPITALS

9 unit word space

1 unit letterspace	LETTERSPACED SMALL CAPITALS
2 unit letterspace	LETTERSPACED SMALL CAPITALS
3 unit letterspace	LETTERSPACED SMALL CAPITALS

1 unit	samplesoffixedwordspacingforlower-case
2 units	samples of fixed word spacing for lower-case
3 units	samples of fixed word spacing for lower-case
4 units	samples of fixed word spacing for lower-case
5 units	samples of fixed word spacing for lower-case
6 units	samples of fixed word spacing for lower-case
7 units	samples of fixed word spacing for lower-case
8 units	samples of fixed word spacing for lower-case
9 units	samples of fixed word spacing for lower-case

ABCDEFGHIJKLMNOPQRSTUVWXYZ ÆŒ &£$
abcdefghijklmnopqrstuvwxyz æœ fiflfffiffl
1234567890 ⅛ ¼ ⅜ ½ ⅝ ¾ ⅞ ⅙ ⅓ ⅔ @ + – × = '''°·% *†‡§‖¶
àèìòù áéíóú âêîôû äëïöü çñ [(.,:;'-'?!—/)]

ABCDEFGHIJKLMNOPQRSTUVWXYZ ÆŒ &£$
abcdefghijklmnopqrstuvwxyz æœ fiflfffiffl
*1234567890 ⅛ ¼ ⅜ ½ ⅝ ¾ ⅞ ⅙ ⅓ ⅔ @ + – × = '''°·% *†‡§‖¶*
àèìòù áéíóú âêîôû äëïöü çñ [(.,:;'-'?!—/)]

ABCDEFGHIJKLMNOPQRSTUVWXYZ ÆŒ &£$
abcdefghijklmnopqrstuvwxyz æœ fiflfffiffl
1234567890 ⅛ ¼ ⅜ ½ ⅝ ¾ ⅞ ⅙ ⅓ ⅔ @ + – × = '''°·% *†‡§‖¶
àèìòù áéíóú âêîôû äëïöü çñ [(.,:;'-'?!—/)]

ABCDEFGHIJKLMNOPQRSTUVWXYZ ÆŒ &£$
abcdefghijklmnopqrstuvwxyz æœ fiflfffiffl
1234567890 ⅛ ¼ ⅜ ½ ⅝ ¾ ⅞ ⅙ ⅓ ⅔ @ + – × = '''°·% *†‡§‖¶
àèìòù áéíóú âêîôû äëïöü çñ [(.,:;'-'?!—/)]

The great advantage of Linotype is the speed with which the composed type is available from the keyboard operation and its ease of handling. Although there are greater restrictions on the number of widths per character than in 'Monotype' this has not seriously hampered the proportions of the letterforms nor the refinements in spacing. Primarily there are only five alphabets of one size available on the keyboard, but 'mixer' machines provide facilities to mix seven or nine alphabets in one or two sizes as shown above.

Linotype differs from single type composition in that the type is set and cast on one machine in one solid line of characters known as a 'slug' (above). The typewriter layout of the keyboard operates a mechanism which assembles matrices in a line from which the slug is cast, the slug is channelled into a galley and the matrices are returned to the assembly line 'bank' ready for re-use.
Both 'Monotype' and 'Linotype' systems cast type from molten lead at speeds up to 1400 words per hour.

ABCDEFGHIJKLMNOPQRSTUVWXYZ

ABCDEFGHIJKLMNOPQRSTUVWXYZ
ABCDEFGHIJKLMNOPQRSTUVWXYZ
ABCDEFGHIJKLMNOPQRSTUVWXYZ
ABCDEFGHIJKLMNOPQRSTUVWXYZ
ABCDEFGHIJKLMNOPQRSTUVWXY
ABCDEFGHIJKLMNOPQRSTU
ABCDEFGHIJKLMNOI

The Monophoto filmsetter is based on the same principle as the Monotype 'hot metal' casting machine. The perforated paper ribbon from a modified keyboard unit controls the film matrix case in the same way. The difference lies in the photographic technique and the system of lenses which allows the negatives from one matrix case (opposite) to be projected to any size between 6pt and 22pt.
The final product of the machine can be on film or paper, as positive or negative, and for reverse reading or direct reading, as required.

In principle, computer-controlled typesetting is not unlike the
'Monotype' system in that a punched paper tape, floppy disc or
magnetic tape is produced on a keyboard unit which subsequently
controls a filmsetting machine. The tape or disc is produced by an
electric typewriter containing an electronic computer and the operator
is able to check his setting from a print-out produced at the same time.
Many systems now incorporate a VDU (Visual Display Unit) for
checking this text entry.
The tapes or discs contain all the coded instructions for the production
units. These can vary from a modified Linotype machine to a high
speed filmsetter and the range of styles and sizes of type available
through most systems is considerably larger than through conventional
ones.

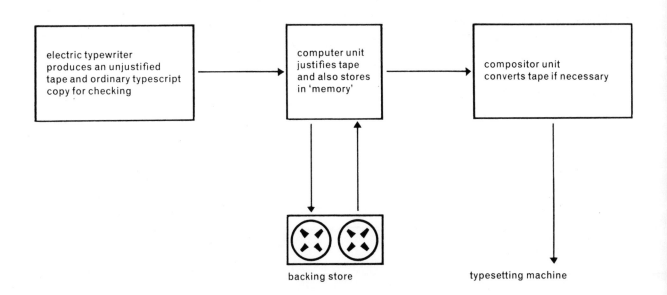

| electric typewriter produces an unjustified tape and ordinary typescript copy for checking | → | computer unit justifies tape and also stores in 'memory' | → | compositor unit converts tape if necessary |

backing store

typesetting machine

Basically, all systems enable the operator to:
1 Key in text material
2 Store an amount of this text
3 Make corrections either before or after typesetting
4 Proof in some form
5 Phototypeset the text
The great advantage which computer-controlled systems have is that the much greater storage and recall facilities enable updating and editing of the text to take place far more easily and quickly than is the case with hot metal or direct impression systems.

The phenomenal speeds of the electronic computer units enable them to handle the output of several keyboard units at the same time and developments are continually taking place in the use of computers throughout the printing industry.
A most important factor for the designer concerns the accuracy and care with which the original copy and layout must be prepared if the process is to be efficient and economical. The designer should acquaint his/her self with the specific requirements of the system to be used. This is particularly difficult due to the rapidly changing technology as new machines are constantly being developed.

ABCDEFGHIJKLMNOPQRSTUVWXYZ
abcdefghijklmnopqrstuvwxyz @ ¼ ¾ ½
! † + £ % / & * ( ) — ' ' : , . ; ? [ ] - =
1234567890

A number of electric typewriters are capable of producing justified lines of 'type' from 6pt to 14pt on paper as a direct image suitable for photographic reproduction. They are easily operated by a typist who types each line twice; the first is unjustified, but, on retyping, the line is automatically justified. A consistent impression is ensured and can be typed on a transluscent paper and used as positive 'film'. The letterforms, word and letterspacing are restricted by the number of different character widths available, but with careful specification this form of 'cold typesetting' (which is comparatively cheap) can produce a good enough imitation of traditional typesetting to deceive the layman.

The two settings below have been prepared on an
IBM Selectric Composer which utilises the 'golf ball head'
(right) in a keyboard unit similar to an electric typewriter.
Each golf ball head contains the alphabets and figures
shown (left) and are very easily interchangeable.

A number of typesetting machines are capable of producing justified lines of 'type' from 6pt to 14pt on paper as a direct image
suitable for photographic reproduction. They are easily operated
by a typist who types each line twice, first as unjustified and then
on retyping, the line is automatically justified. A consistent impression is controlled and can be typed on a translucent paper and
used as positive 'film'. The letterforms, word and letter spacing
are restricted by the number of different character widths available but with careful specification this form of 'cold typesetting'
(which is comparatively cheap) can produce a good enough imitation of traditional typesetting to deceive the layman.

A number of typesetting machines are capable of producing justified lines of 'type' from 6pt to 14pt on paper as a direct image
suitable for photographic reproduction. They are easily operated
by a typist who types each line twice, first as unjustified and then
on retyping, the line is automatically justified. A consistent impression is controlled and can be typed on a translucent paper and
used as positive 'film'. The letterforms, word and letter spacing
are restricted by the number of different character widths available but with careful specification this form of 'cold typesetting'
(which is comparatively cheap) can produce a good enough imitation of traditional typesetting to deceive the layman.

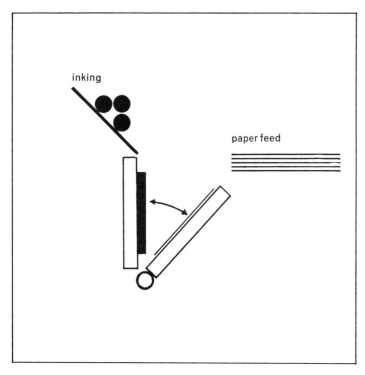

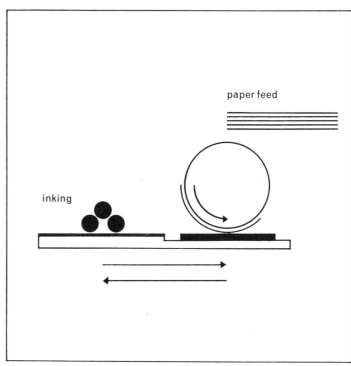

The platen press is a letterpress machine which holds the type flat and prints on to the paper flat. The area of type matter which can be printed is limited as the pressure must be even over the whole surface and it is difficult to maintain this sufficiently above a certain area. The illustration shows the type held vertically; paper is fed on to the hinged platen which is closed to bring the type and paper into contact. Inking takes place as the platen opens and closes.

This type of press is capable of very precise work and is suitable for a wide variety of ephemeral print.

Cylinder presses are capable of printing letterpress over a larger area as they bring the paper into contact with flat type at only one point along the cylinder, requiring considerably less overall pressure than the platen type.

The sheets of paper are drawn tight round the cylinder as it rolls over the type and inking is automatically controlled to intersperse with each revolution.

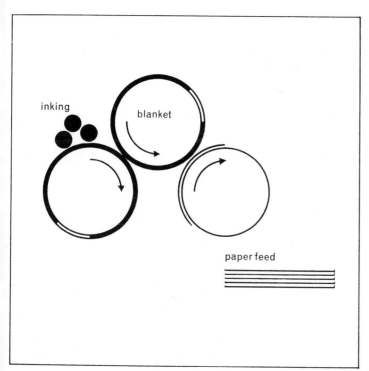

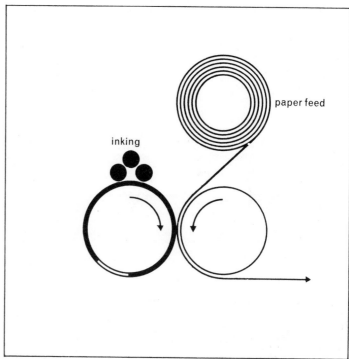

Printing from a rotary press is basically the same in letterpress and offset-litho. Paper can be fed in single sheets or from a continuous 'web' as in newspaper work (hence, 'web-offset'). The diagram shows the roll of paper being fed on to the impression cylinder and brought into contact with the plate which has already been inked. Letterpress surfaces are duplicated from an original conventional relief surface and made into a flexible plate which is wrapped round the cylinder.

The thin metal plates used for lithography enable them to be wrapped round a cylinder, the image is offset on to a rubber blanket and from there on to paper which is pressed against the blanket by the impression cylinder. The softness of the rubber blanket enables the image to be printed effectively on paper with quite an uneven surface as well as a variety of surfaces such as tin or plastic (contrast letterpress).

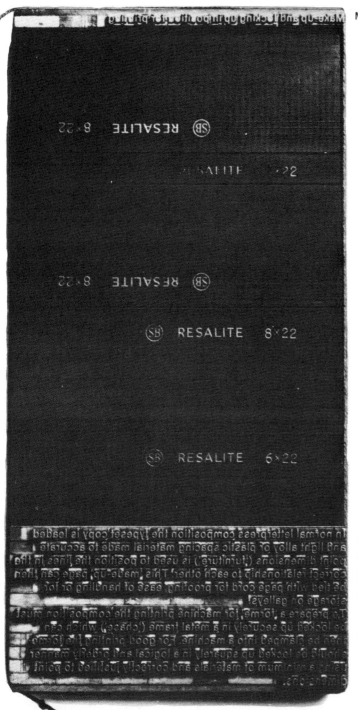

In normal letterpress composition the typeset copy is leaded and light alloy or plastic spacing material made to accurate point dimensions ('furniture') is used to position the lines in the correct relationship to each other. This 'made-up' page can then be tied with page cord for proofing, ease of handling or for storage on galleys.

To prepare a 'forme' for machine printing the composition must be locked up securely in a metal frame ('chase') which can then be clamped into a machine. For good printing the forme should be locked up squarely in a logical and orderly manner using a minimum of materials and correctly justified to point dimensions.

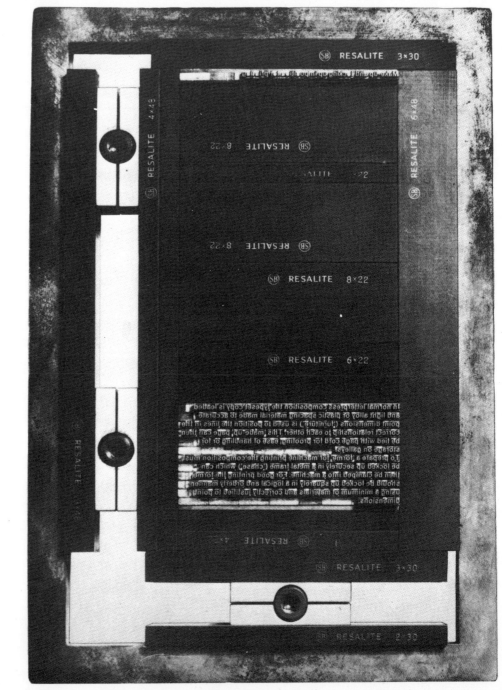

Filmset copy is prepared for reproduction on a light box or 'make-up table', which enables the operator to see the image easily. Proofs of typesetting pulled on opaque white bromide paper can be made up for camera work by normal artwork procedures, but film is positioned accurately using a film backing sheet which adheres by contact. Parallel rulers and set squares are used to ensure the film is mounted correctly and this temporary assembly of material can be 'proofed' through a photo-copying or 'Diazo' type machine and corrections made on the light box before finalizing the position with adhesive tape.

Ɛ	9	S	ⱱ
2	7	8	1

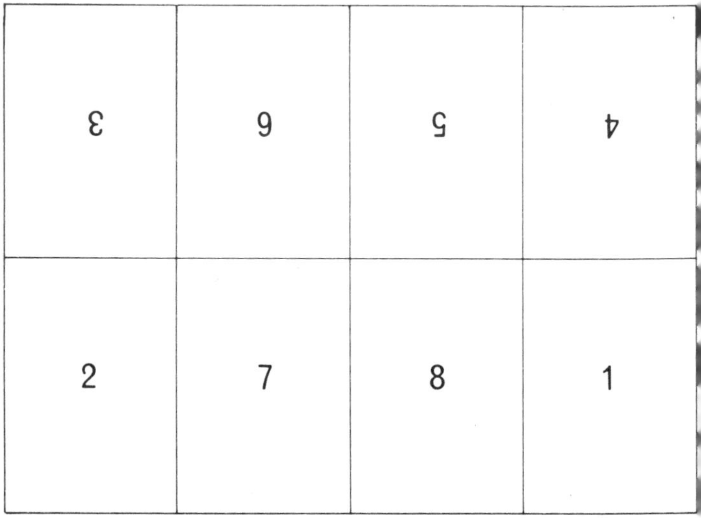

Several pages of a book or magazine, etc, are printed at the same time irrespective of printing process. The way in which the paper is to be folded by the folding machine available dictates how these pages are assembled for them to be printed in the right order.
The diagram shows one possible arrangement – a sixteen-page 'imposition' which is folded systematically in half four times; the illustration opposite is of an eight-page imposition of letterpress material.

Symmetrical design
is the
traditional use of space
within a frame
balanced on a central
axis

Asymmetrical design
utilises the total area within a frame
creating an off-centre balance

The classic typographic layout centres each line on each other and is positioned centrally in the page area. The type is treated in the same manner as a classical painting – one sees into the painting as through a window. The lines stand out as 'foreground' and the white space as merely background.

The modern asymmetric layout derives its principles from the change in attitudes towards painting at the beginning of this century when the canvas was treated as a flat surface, the 'background' assuming equal importance with the foreground.
The whole of the area is used, including the edge of the 'frame', which creates an off-centre balance.

Asymmetrical design
may be informal, where
the lines of type are positioned
by the designer's intuition

A formal asymmetrical
design is achieved
by placing the lines of type
in a non-arbitrary
position which divides
the area mathematically

Asymmetric principles allow considerably more freedom to the designer who may place the lines of type where he pleases, the only limit being the legibility of the copy. Lines which create an off-centre balance but are positioned arbitrarily are asymmetric but 'informal'.

The logical and mathematical division of an area in horizontal and vertical proportions explored by artists such as Mondrian is directly related to typography. Lines of type naturally form horizontal and vertical planes which subdivide the page. The function of most printed matter is to present the copy in a clear and logical sequence; the formal, non-arbitrary method of dividing the page is a suitable form in which to present factual copy.

A considerable amount of confusion has arisen due to the freedom of asymmetric typography. The classical tradition has a simple formula of balancing the elements in a layout equally on a central axis, so that the copy can be easily divided into lines and groups and fall naturally along this axis. The methods of arranging copy asymmetrically are more varied but just as logical.

The off-centred 'axis' can be drawn in any position within the page area, determined by the designer's intuition or by non-arbitrary, mathematical means (for example, the line above is 1:3). Lines of type centred on such an axis would have a disturbing effect, but when the line is 'drawn' by aligning lines of type at that point the division is obvious to the eye.

Typographic
division of an area

Groups of type
aligned at one side
create an effect
of vertical lines

Each group forms
a column read
from left to right

The page area may be divided several times by vertical lines according to the requirements of the copy and there are many aesthetic variations which the designer may invent.
Most design requirements, however, usually involve the complex factors of visual continuity, production techniques and cost, quite apart from the nature of the message to be communicated, and the designer has to incorporate all these requirements into his method of layout.

In the example above (left) an area is divided into three and a typographic adaptation of this basic pattern is shown above (right). Typography is read from left to right and top to bottom and this principle is employed in the new layout technique, by dividing the page area into the same number of divisions as there are naturally in the copy.
The size and weight of the type need not necessarily be varied as the groups are placed in order of importance from the left.

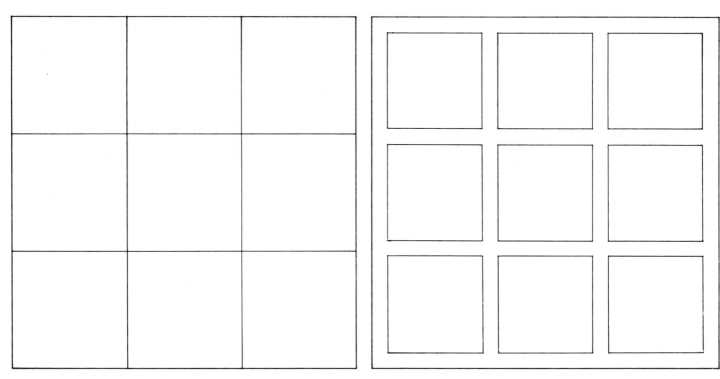

An area may be divided up into vertical and horizontal sections which create a network or 'grid'. A square unit similar to the one above is one of the most common bases of a grid system; it allows a considerable manipulation of the units without losing the underlying pattern, particularly on a range of separate items where visual continuity is required.

Although the page area is divided up over the whole of the surface, it is unpractical to print type on the edge of the paper, and columns of type also require a space between them, so the basic network is adapted for typographic purposes by allowing a small margin between each division.

The grid shown above is drawn to point dimensions necessary to accommodate typographic material (6 em squares plus 1 em margins).

<table>
<tr><td>

Use of space

Typographic   A modular grid
                               of squares is
                               the formal basis

                    Taken in sequence
                    each group of type
                    is allotted a
                    position which is
                    determined by
                    the underlying grid

</td><td>

Adaptability

Copy of less   Elements of varying quality,
importance may
be set smaller   texture and tone may be

                    composed together using

                    the same grid, each element

                    taking up an area or areas

                    according to their

                    importance and relationship

                    to each other within the page

</td></tr>
</table>

The grid on the previous page has been employed here to distribute the typeset copy over the area, and the eye is guided from one group to the next by its position and the condition of reading left to right, head to foot.

Lines of type at the extremes of the grid 'identify' with the edge of the page and if too wide a margin is allowed a traditional 'border' effect may confuse the underlying design principles. The margin is as close as the production technique will permit.

The tremendous advantage of the grid system is its adaptability – elements which are inherently very different in shape, size, texture, etc, can be given a visually unified relationship within the same frame and succeeding items can also be related to each other. It should be noted that the grid is not a preconceived plan into which everything must be forced, but a formula which *evolves from the material itself* – a result of visually co-ordinating varying elements, usually for the purpose of standardizing them for production.

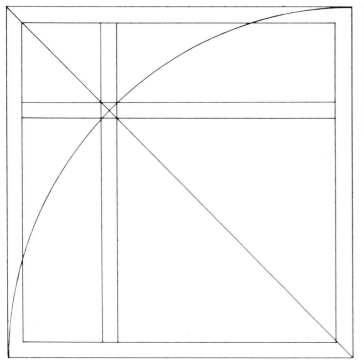

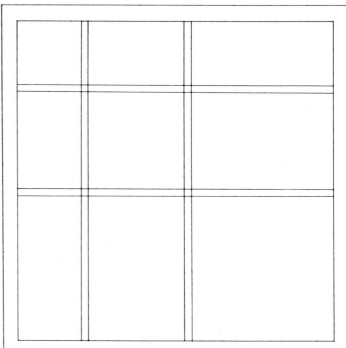

In devising a grid, the designer has to rationalize the nature of his message and 'materials' to be presented, in relation to visual concepts and production methods. It is not within the scope of this book to examine the first requirement, but it is relevant to the designer to be familiar with purely visual methods of constructing grids.
The drawing above shows a grid constructed on the 'golden section' proportion.

Three divisions of an increasing ratio of 2–3–4 units (ems) present a system which has a great many combinations of related proportions.

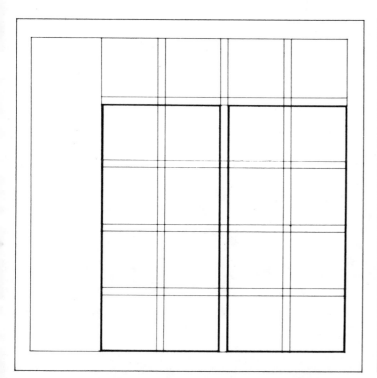

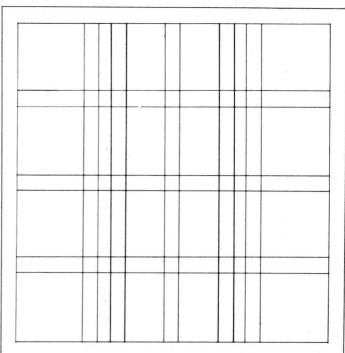

In the majority of design projects the grid is determined not only by the character of the visual units to be incorporated, but also by the technical constraints imposed by the production method.
For example, pages in a loose-leaf binder require a minimum inner margin to allow for the ring binding. The grid above allows for this and two columns of type matter, a head margin and proportional breakdown into units for photographs, etc. The outside margins are slightly larger to allow for some variation in the trimming, but all the margins are in proportion to all the other elements within the page.

Columns of type in newpaper and magazine work divide the page into vertical sections, and the number of columns is limited only by the minimum width of a line of type for a comfortable reading length. Different sizes of type may allow different widths to be employed in the same series and the same page. Grids of this type allow maximum freedom in the individual page layout but require careful handling to be successful.

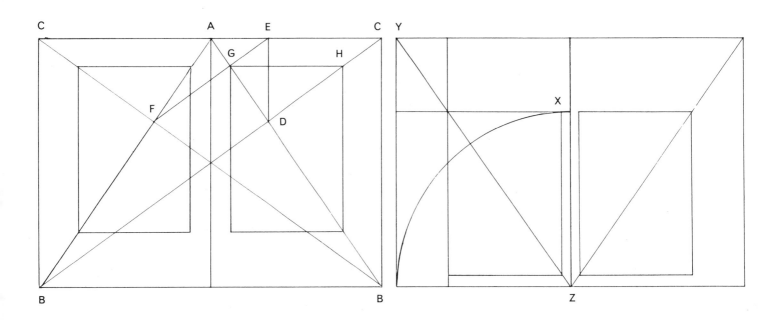

·A method of determining the type area and margins has been used traditionally for centuries and it is only in recent years that the term 'grid system' has been used to describe this technique usually applied to modern design formats.

The diagram shows the classical proportions of type area to margins based on the diagonals A–B. The double page diagonal B–C gives point D, a vertical is drawn to the top of the page (E) and the line E–F is completed. Where this line crosses the diagonal at G gives the height of the type area, and a horizontal to H enables the full type area to be drawn in. The inner (gutter) margin is two units, the head is three units, the foredge is four units and the foot margin is five units.

The margins of a 'modern' book of the same size and type area are arrived at by a simpler use of the space; the diagonal Y–Z is drawn and the point X is fixed by drawing a horizontal at the same distance from the foot as the width of the page (the 'golden section') and where this meets the diagonal determines the type width.

There appears to be more white margin because it is concentrated in only two areas; the inner and foot margins 'identify' with the edge of the page having been reduced to the technical minimum required for production.

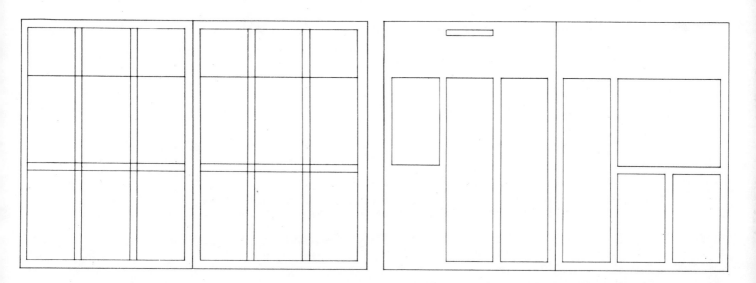

Magazines and catalogues normally demand a greater number of columns and adaptability for different size illustrations and the grid above is an example of a simple three-column grid with horizontal divisions to allocate a constant head margin and illustration areas.

The application of this grid has a great number of variations to suit individual page requirements. The illustrations may vary from the smallest rectangle through any combination of them to the full page size. Columns of type economically set to a constant width are easily balanced with the illustrations and margins. It is desirable for most catalogues, etc, to have a logical basis for the organization of the contents both for the reader's comprehension and ease of production. If, however, too many pages become too monotonous then the occasional contrast of an informally placed heading or 'free' illustration helps to enliven the severity of the formal basis.

The most accurate way to estimate how many lines of type a given piece of copy will make when set in type is by the Character Count method which is based on the average number of characters each typeface contains in a specific length of line. The total number of letters and spaces are counted in each paragraph and this sum is divided by the number of characters in the typeface and length of line required, which indicates the number of lines.

measure in ems	10	12	14	16	18	20	22
6pt	39	47	55	63	70	78	86
8pt	32	39	45	51	58	64	71
10pt	26	32	37	42	48	53	58
12pt	22	26	31	35	40	44	49

Example 1
The copy is to be set in 10pt Baskerville U/L, to 22 ems measure, (3pt lead).
437 characters divided by 58 make 8 lines.

Example 2
The copy is to be set in 8pt Baskerville U/L, to 11 ems measure fixed word space ('unjustified') ranged left 2pt lead.
437 characters divided by 35 make 13 lines.

Casting-off is the term given to the mathematical conversion of lines of copy into lines of type. The simplest method is to estimate the number of words in the copy and multiply this by six (the average word in English prose contains five letters plus one space) which represents the total number of 'characters' If a more accurate cast-off is essential, then the quickest way to count the actual number of characters is to draw a line down through the typewritten copy level with the shortest line. Typewritten characters are normally the same width. The number contained in this shortest line is multiplied by the number of lines and the remainder are counted individually and added to arrive at a total.

Most typefounders supply casting-off charts (similar to the table above) representing the average number of characters each typeface contains in a line.
The typographer selects the size and measure he wishes to set the type in, reads the number indicated on the chart and divides this into the total number of characters. (Whenever there are 'remainders', these constitute the last short line of paragraphs).
The two examples above are shown opposite as typesettings.

The most accurate way to estimate how many lines of type a given piece of copy will make when set in type is by the Character Count method which is based on the average number of characters each typeface contains in a specific length of line. The total number of letters and spaces are counted in each paragraph and this sum is divided by the number of characters in the typeface and length of line required, which indicates the number of lines

The most accurate way to estimate how many lines of type a given piece of copy will make when set in type is by the Character Count method which is based on the average number of characters each typeface contains in a specific length of line. The total number of letters and spaces are counted in each paragraph and this sum is divided by the number of characters in the typeface and length of line required, which indicates the number of lines

The most accurate way to estimate how many lines of type a given piece of/copy will make when set in type is by the Character Count method/which is based on the average number of characters each typeface contains in a specific length of line. The total/ number of letters and spaces are counted in each/paragraph and this sum is divided by the/number of characters in the type-/ face and the length of line/required, which indicates/the total number/of lines.

The most accurate way to estimate how many lines of type a given piece of copy will make when set in type is by the Character Count method which is based on the average number of characters each type-face contains in a specific length of line. The total number of letters and spaces are counted in each paragraph and this sum is divided by the number of characters in the type-face and the length of line required, which indicates the total number of lines

The typographer often has to fit copy into a confined area or he may wish to prepare a layout showing the exact length of lines, etc. The inserting of extra space between words to fit artistic shapes is rarely justified but breaking naturally-spaced lines at points to integrate the type into a composition is often required in publicity design. Each line is counted individually and the length can be marked on a layout accurately and adjusted until the best shape is reached; each line is marked in the copy by a diagonal stroke.

The setting above is an arbitrary shape to demonstrate the markings in the copy on the left.

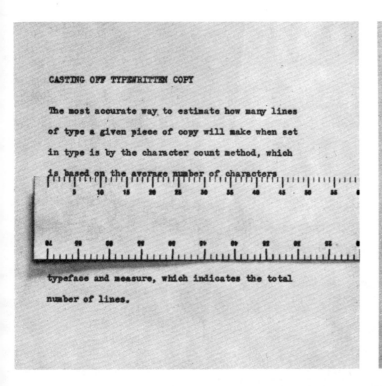

CASTING OFF TYPEWRITTEN COPY

The most accurate way to estimate how many lines of type a given piece of copy will make when set in type is by the character count method, which is based on the average number of characters

typeface and measure, which indicates the total number of lines.

The most accurate way to estimate how many Lines of type a given piece of copy will make when set in type is by the Character Count principle, which is based on the average number of characters each typeface contains in a specific length of line. The total number of letters and spaces are counted in each paragraph and this sum is divided by the number of characters in the typeface and measure, which indicates the number of lines.

| 10 point | 10 | 20 | 30 | 40 | 50 | 60 |
| | 1234567890 | 1234567890 | 1234567890 | 1234567890 | 1234567890 | 1234567890123 |

| 12 point | 10 | 20 | 30 | 40 | 50 | |
| | 1234567890 | 1234567890 | 1234567890 | 1234567890 | 1234567890 | 123 |

The laborious task of counting characters in copy can be eased by two simple devices illustrated here.
The standard typewriter has characters of equal width, either ten characters or twelve characters per inch, and a 'typewriter measure' can easily be made indicating both sizes. This scale is laid on to the line of typescript and the total can be read off very quickly.

The illustration above shows the type of scale used above left actually printed in a light grey on the copy paper. As the typist taps out the copy the number of characters can be read off the scale at the foot of the page. All the copy must be typed from the left-hand edge.
This method is very useful for magazine copy for example, as the type-set measure is probably known and the typist can type the copy to the required width, thus 'automatically' casting off the copy so that the typographer needs only to count the number of lines.

Manuscripts and typewritten copy which are supplied to the keyboard operator for machine typesetting must be carefully read, and marked accordingly, to correct any inconsistencies of punctuation, subtitling, etc. The editing for grammatical 'style' is a very important aspect of designing for print and full instructions for spacing, position and length of lines, weight and fount (font), etc, must be indicated throughout the typescript copy (see 'proof corrections' for symbols).

TYPOGRAPHIC STYLE FOR TEXT COMPOSITION ← *bold u/L*

n.p. full out

← Lines of type for continuous reading should contain on average between ten and twelve words, closely and evenly word spaced with clear interlinear space. Paragraphs should be indicated by indentingone em of the type size used but the first paragraph of each new section should be set full out.

#

In roman typefaces words set in capitals and small capitals should be letterspaced and small caps are better than caps when lines within containing lower-case.

□

no extra leading
full out
n.p. full out

← Punctuation *bold u/L*

← Punctuation should be kept to a minimum and only used to avoid possible confusion providing the use is consistent throughout the text.   Full points are not necessary after well known abbreviations and contractions, for example, Mr, Mrs, Messrs, Dr, Co, Ltd, St, WC2, etc, 8vo, cwt, lb, s(shillings), d(pence)/. In abbreviated qualifications, titles, etc., where two or more are set together omit the last full point, for example, M.S.I.A, M.S.T.D.   Full points may be omitted entirely in display if they are not likely to be confused.

∂/ ,

The same word space (visually) as that used throughout the rest of the line should follow punctuation with no extra space at the end of a sentence.

□

Single quotations marks are adequate to indicate 'speech' or references to other texts - double quotes are used for quotes within quotes - where quotations are shown in italics or a smaller size of type, quotation marks are not necessary.

□
single Quotes

In place of em rules (—), use en rules (-), preceded and followed by a word space.

□

full out
n.p. full out

← Hyphenation *bold u/L*

← Where it is necessary to break words at the ends of lines, the division should be made phonetically, for example, typog-raphy, method-ical. Words containing double consanants are divided by splitting them, for example, syl-lable, set-ting.

A layout for the composing room does not have to be as highly finished as a design presented for a client's approval, but it does have to be accurate and clearly indicate the type faces to be used and measurements. Basically the same information which is specified on the copy sheet must be shown on the layout also and each part of the copy must be clearly identified.

All the dimensions must be worked out on the point scale and the instructions marked at the side, on the layout or as an overlay, depending on which is the clearest method.

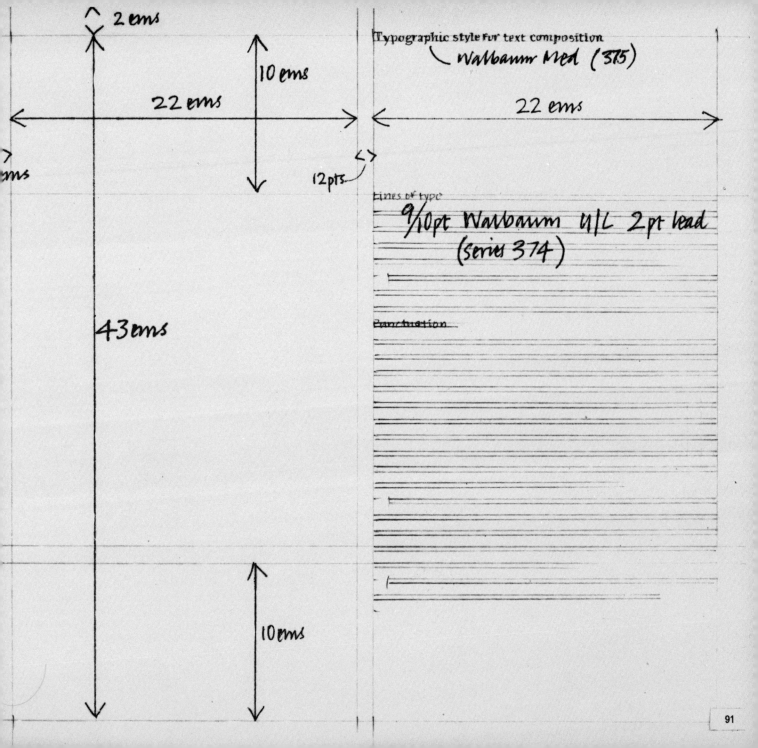

2 ems

10 ems

22 ems

22 ems

Typographic style for text composition

Walbaum Med (375)

12 pts

Lines of type

9/10pt Walbaum U/L 2 pt lead
(series 374)

43 ems

Punctuation

10 ems

Typesetting for continuous reading should not be visually eccentric but within the bounds of 'acceptability' of the reader; that which is acceptable usually means that which is familiar. There are physiological factors, however, which are fairly constant; for example, the length of line for comfortable reading and the relationship of space between the words and lines. To convey information with clarity and speed the setting should be consistent in the use of punctuation and of related founts (fonts) of type which give the different 'tones of voice' to the printed language. The two settings opposite show the difference between an inconsistent and badly spaced setting and one which is logically styled and carefully spaced.

Lines of type for continuous reading should contain on average between ten and twelve words, closeley and evenly word spaced with clear interlinear space. Paragraphs should be indicated by indenting one em of the type size used but the first paragraph of each new section should be set full out.

In roman typefaces words set in CAPITALS and SMALL CAPITALS should be letterspaced and small capitals are better than capitals when used within lines containing lower-case.

PUNCTUATION

Punctuation should be kept to a minimum and only used to avoid possible confusion providing it is consistent throughout the text. Full points are not necessary after well-known abbreviations and contractions, for example, Mr., Mrs., Messrs., Dr., Co., Ltd., St., WC2., etc., 8vo., cwt., lb., s. (shillings) d. (pence). In abbreviated qualifications, titles, etc, where two or more are set together, omit the last full point, for example, M.S.I.A., M.S.T.D. Full points may be omitted entirely in display where the abbreviations are not likely to be confused. The same word space (visually) as that used throughout the rest of the line should follow punctuation with no extra space at the end of a sentence.

Single quotation marks are adequate to indicate ''speech'' or references to other texts—double quotes are only used for quotations within quotations—where quotations are shown in italics or a smaller size of type, quotation marks are not necessary.

In place of em rules (—) use en rules (–), preceded and followed by a word space.

Lines of type for continuous reading should contain on average between ten and twelve words, closely and evenly word spaced with clear interlinear space. Paragraphs should be indicated by indenting one em of the type size used but the first paragraph of each new section should be set full out.

In roman typefaces words set in CAPITALS and SMALL CAPITALS should be letterspaced and small capitals are better than capitals when used within lines containing lower-case.

Punctuation

Punctuation should be kept to a minimum and only used to avoid possible confusion providing it is consistent throughout the text. Full points are not necessary after well-known abbreviations and contractions, for example, Mr, Mrs, Messrs, Dr, Co, Ltd, St, WC2, etc, 8vo, cwt, lb, s (shillings) d (pence). In abbreviated qualifications, titles, etc, where two or more are set together, omit the last full point, for example, M.S.I.A, M.S.T.D. Full points may be omitted entirely in display where the abbreviations are not likely to be confused. The same word space (visually) as that used throughout the rest of the line should follow punctuation with no extra space at the end of a sentence.

Single quotation marks are adequate to indicate 'speech' or references to other texts – double quotes are only used for quotations within quotations – where quotations are shown in italics or a smaller size of type, quotation marks are not necessary.

In place of em rules (—) use en rules (–), preceded and followed by a word space.

text mark		marginal mark	meaning
⋏		new matter followed by /	insert
⌀⟋		strike through unwanted letter/s	delete
⋯⋯	under characters	*stet*	leave as printed
____	under characters	*ital*	change to italics
═══	under characters	*s.c.*	change to small caps
≡≡≡	under characters	*caps*	change to caps
∿∿∿	under characters	*bold*	change to bold type
	encircle letter/s	*l.c.*	change to lower-case
	encircle letter/s	*rom*	change to roman
	encircle letter/s	*w.f.*	wrong fount
	encircle letter/s	⊘	invert type
	encircle letter/s	✗	change damaged type

text mark		marginal mark	meaning
⌣	linking characters	⌣	close up
⋏		#	insert space
⁄⁄⁄⁄⁄	between top of letters	*letter* #	letterspace
⌐⌐	around letters	*trs*	transpose
⌐		☐	indent one em
⊏		⊏⊐	indent two ems
[ ]	around letters	*move*	move to the position indicated
⌒	between paragraphs	*run on*	no new paragraph
⊏	before first word	*n.p.*	begin new paragraph
⊤	over and under lines	*raise*	raise lines
⊥	over and under lines	*lower*	lower lines
>	between lines	*2pts*	insert leading (2pts)

A code of signs and abbreviations is fairly universal to printers and the chart above shows the most common and useful marks for the designer in specifying layouts and correcting proofs.

Corrections are shown in the margins of proofs and where there is more than one error in a line each mark is separated by a diagonal line and read from left to right in sequence with the marks in the text.

full out

x/x/

l.c.

letter #

full out / bold

full out

o/

,/

,/

Cap

□/single quotes

trs

2 pts

Lines of type for continuous reading should contain on average between ten and twelve words, closely and evenly word spaced with clear interlinear space. Paragraphs should be indicated by indenting one em of the type size used but the first Paragraph of each new section should be set full out.

In roman typefaces words set in CAPITALS and SMALL CAPITALS should be letterspaced and small capitals are better than capitals when used within lines containing lower-case.

Punctuation

Punctuation should be kept to a minimum and only used to avoid possible confusion providing it is consistent throughout the text. Full points are not necessary after well-known abbreviations and contractions, for example Mr, Mrs, Messrs, Dr, Co, Ltd, St, WC2, etc, 8vo, cwt, lb, s (shillings) d (pence). In abbreviated qualifications, titles, etc, where two or more are set together, omit the last full point, for example, M.S.I.A, M.S.T.D. Full points may be omitted entirely in display where the abbreviations are not likely to be confused. the same word space (visually) as that used throughout the rest of the line should follow punctuation with no extra space at the end of a sentence.

Single quotation marks are adequate to indicate 'speech' or references to other texts – double quotes only are used for quotations within quotations – where quotations are shown in italics or a smaller size of type, quotation marks are not necessary.

In place of em rules (—) use en rules (–), preceded and followed by a word space.

Art Board (or **paper**) Called coated paper in the USA, board or paper coated with china clay giving a very smooth surface, mostly used in letterpress for printing half-tones.

Ascenders The portion of letters in lower-case (non-capitals) which extends above the height of the 'x' – in the letters b d f h k l t.

Base-line The imaginary line on which the base of a letter stands.

Binding The process of assembling pages and fixing covers to books.

Blanket The packing used on the impression cylinder of a printing machine – it may be made of paper, cloth or rubber.

Bold face A type of heavier appearance than the normal reading weight.

Case A tray divided into small compartments to contain quantities of the various characters in a fount (font) of type. Hence, upper-case (capitals) and lower-case.

Calligraphy The art of writing.

Characters Individual type letters, figures and punctuation marks, etc.

Compositor A person trained to set type.

Descenders The portion of letters in lower-case which hangs below the base line – in the letters g j p y q.

Die-case Another name for the 'Monotype' matrix case.

Forme The assembly of type and spaces locked up in a metal chase, ready for printing.

Fount (font) All the characters of a type design – alphabets of capitals, lower-case, figures, punctuation.

Galley A flat metal tray used to make-up and store type.

Image The term used to describe the subject represented for reproduction.

Italic Usually types which slope to the right and are based on cursive handwriting, used as 'companion' types to roman alphabets.

Jobbing printing A term given to commercial printing other than newspaper and bookwork.

Legibility The speed and accuracy with which type may be read.

Lower-case The 'small' letters normally used for continuous reading – the non-capitals (sometimes referred to as minuscules).

Matrix A metal die from which type characters are cast.

Page area The overall dimensions of a page in a book including the white margins as well as the type area.

Pica Another name for the 12pt em.

Punch An engraving of a type character from which the matrices are made.

Register The correct position for printing typematter.

Scripts A letterform based on the cursive handwriting made with a quill pen.

Serifs The decorative small strokes at the ends of letters.

Small capitals An alphabet of capital letters (available in most roman types) which are approximately the same height as the lower-case 'x'.

Text Continuous reading copy.

Type area The area taken up by the type on a page.

Upper-case The capital letters in a fount (font).

Wrong fount (font) An error in typesetting caused by a letterform from another typeface becoming mixed in the case.